I Am in Foster Care, But I Am Not Alone

An Introduction to Foster Care Helpers

I Am in Foster Care, But I Am Not Alone

An Introduction to Foster Care Helpers

By Kate Hlava

Disclaimer:
This book is a work of fiction Any resemblance to actual persons, living or dead, is purely coincidental. The roles and situations depicted are general representations and are not intended to portray specific individuals.

Printed in the United States of America

Preface

Every child deserves to feel safe, loved, and cared for. But sometimes, families face challenges that make it hard for them to give children what they need. When that happens, foster care can step in — not as a replacement for family, but as a circle of grown-ups who work together to keep children safe and supported.

This book was written to help children in foster care understand the many caring adults who are a part of their lives: foster parents, the family they were born into, social workers, therapists, judges, attorneys, CASA volunteers, and more. Each one has a special role, but they all share the same goal — to make sure children are healthy, safe, and never alone.

The story follows Logan, a child like so many others in foster care, who learns that even though foster care can feel confusing and scary at times, there is a team of people who care deeply and want the best for her. Use this book to start conversations, answer questions, and remind children that they are not alone.

Every kid needs love and care.

Sometimes kids need extra helpers too—
grown-ups who make sure we are safe,
healthy, and happy.

I'm Logan, and this is the story of the special helpers
in my life.

I live with my **foster parents.** They give me a safe place to sleep, yummy meals to eat, and hugs when I need them.

Foster parents aren't the same as my mom or dad,
but they take care of me every day. They love and
care for me while I am here.

I also have **the family I was born into**.

That means the people who were there when I came into the world—like my mom, my dad, or other family members.
They gave me my very first hugs and smiles.

Even if I don't live with them right now, they are still a special part of me. Sometimes I get to see them or talk to them. Sometimes I can't. But they are always in my heart.

My helpers talk with the family I was born into too, to help figure out what keeps me safe and happy.

I can love the family I was born into and the family I live with now—both at the same time.

My **social worker** is a helper. They ask me how I'm feeling and really listen to me. They also talk with my foster parents, the family I was born into, and the other helpers who care about me.

They take me to visits and appointments. But their biggest job is to make sure I am safe, cared for, and never forgotten.

Police officers are helpers too.

If there is danger, they make sure kids get to a safe place.

They help my social worker. They help families too.

Their job is to protect people.

Police officers are part of my team.

.

I might feel sad. I might feel mad. I might feel scared.

My **therapist** helps me. We can play, draw,or use toys
to tell my story.

They remind me:
Every feeling is okay.
Feelings don't last forever.
Love always stays.

I have a helper for court. She is called an **attorney.** Her job is to speak up for me. She tells the judge what I need and how I feel. She helps make sure my voice is heard.

Sometimes my helper for court is called a CASA - That means Court Appointed Special Avocate. A CASA is a grown-up who spends time wiht me, listens to me, and then tells the judge what life is like for me.

A **judge** is a very important helper.

They sit in a big chair, behind a big desk called the bench.

The judge listens to everyone:
my social worker,
my foster parents,
the family I was born into,
and my attorney or CASA.

Then the judge decides what is safest and best for me.

All these helpers are part of my team

.They don't all do the same job, but they work together— for me.

They want me to be safe. They want me to grow strong. They want me to know I matter.

Sometimes I wonder why there are so many grown-ups in my life.

But then I remember:
Each one is here because they care about me.
Each one is here to help me.
They are my team.

And no matter what,
I am important.
I am special.
I am loved.

Questions Kids Often Ask About Being In Foster Care

Psst... want to know a secret?
When I first came into foster care, I had so many questions. Maybe you have some too.
Whenever I asked my helpers, their answers helped me feel calmer. The questions that follow are some of mine—
 nd maybe they're yours too.

Psst... one more thing.
It's always okay to have more questions. I still think of new ones all the time!
And guess what? You can keep asking your helpers—again, and again, and again.
Because your questions matter.
And you matter most of all.

Logan

Sometimes parents need extra help. Foster care is a safe place for kids to stay while the grown-ups get the help they need.

Did I do something wrong?

No. Being in foster care is never a kid's fault. It's the
grown-ups' job to keep kids safe. You did nothing wrong.

Will I see my family again?

Most of the time, yes. Kids in foster care usually get to see their families. Sometimes visits happen at a special place, with a helper close by.

Every story is different. Helpers—like the judge and
social worker— talk with each other to keep you safe
while they figure out what's best.

Do people really care about me?

Yes. Lots of people love and care about you and they
are on your team making sure you're safe and loved.

A Note from the Author

Dear Reader,

This book was created with one hope in mind: that children in foster care feel seen, safe, and loved as they turn these pages. Foster care can bring many changes and questions, but it can also bring caring helpers who want the very best for you.

If you are a child reading this book, I want you to know—you matter. You are important. You are loved.

If you are a caregiver, foster parent, or helper reading along, thank you for walking beside a child with tenderness and care. Your presence makes a difference.

With love and hope,

Kate

www.ingramcontent.com/pod-product-compliance
Lightning Source LLC
Chambersburg PA
CBHW041130120626
46547CB00019B/2937